Pink Magic

The Book of Shadows: Pink Edition

Brittany Nightshade

Nightshade Apothecary Publishing

Table of Contents

Preface 5

Circle Casting 7

Joyful Heart Cleansing 11

Embracing Inner Beauty 14

Serene Sleep Spell 17

Yoruba Waters of Love 20

Blossoming Confidence 23

Bonds of Friendship 26

Faerie's Slumber 29

Aphrodite's Ritual of Self Love 32

Inner Goddess Empowerment 36

Brigid's Healing Bath 39

Abundance and Prosperity 43

Activating Inner Strength 46

Quan Yin's Healing Heart Ritual 50

Moonlit Manifestations of Selene 53

Yoruba Energy Cleanse 57

Creative Inspiration Ritual 60

Blooming Confidence 64

Hecate's Liminal Dreamcraft 68

Lunar Blessings of Chang'e 73

Tiamat's Salt Soak for Radiant Skin 77

Floral Blessings of Flora 82

Love Talisman 85

Athena's Mirror 91

Garden of Gratitude 96

Melodic Muse 100

Rhythms of Friendship 105

In Closing 109

Preface

Welcome to the grimoire of Pink Magic, a book that invites you to embrace the power of positivity, love, and harmony through delightful rituals. This magical guide will take you on a journey of self-discovery, where you can tap into the magic within and infuse your life with joy, serenity, and a touch of pink enchantment.

Within these pages, you will find an array of rituals designed to uplift your spirits and create a sense of wonder in your everyday life. "Pink Magic" is not your traditional magic book; it's a lighthearted and joy-filled exploration of rituals that celebrate the beauty of life, harness the energy of love, and nurture your soul.

In the hustle and bustle of our modern world, it's easy to get caught up in the challenges and pressures that surround us. This grimoire offers a respite—a sanctuary where you can let go of worries and immerse yourself in a world of positive intention and gentle enchantment.

The rituals shared in this book are crafted with care and infused with the intention to bring happiness, self-validation, and feminine strength into your life. Whether you're seeking solace from sadness, yearning for a boost of confidence, or desiring a deeper connection with your inner self.

In this book you will encounter a variety of goddesses, each radiating their unique qualities and energies. Through invoking their presence, you can align yourself with their wisdom, grace, and power. These rituals honor the divine feminine within and empower you to embrace your own inner magic.

So, whether you're a seasoned practitioner or just beginning to explore the world of magic, "Pink Magic" is here to inspire you, uplift your spirits, and ignite your imagination. Embrace the sweetness, the love, and the harmonious energy that awaits you within these pages. Let this book of shadows be your guide as you embark on a delightful journey of self-discovery and enchantment.

Are you ready to paint your world with hues of pink and infuse your life with positivity? Let's embark on this magical adventure together!

Circle Casting

Witches may cast a circle to prepare a magical, sacred space to meditate, cast a spell or perform a ritual. The circles are actually spheres that are used as a type of insulation from unwanted energies which might affect the spell, ritual, or meditation. This helps prevent the misdirection of intention during spell work or the interruption of energy transference. Circles aren't necessary, but in my opinion, can greatly aid in concentration.

A circle can be cast by simply holding out your finger, wand, athame or staff and turning 360 degrees in a clockwise motion. The circle can be closed after you are done by doing the same but in reverse (counterclockwise) or by cutting the boundary of the circle with your athame, wand, or hand. This is an easy and effective way to cast a circle, but you might also wish to incorporate an invocation or ritual of your own design. It doesn't matter how you cast your circle; the key is having faith in what you are doing so you can effectively use your energy to create the barrier.

A popular method of casting a circle involves incorporating the elements and cardinal directions into the casting. For example, you might want to place an object representing each element in each direction you will be pointing to while casting the circle or call upon the guardians and elements themselves. The following are examples of what might be used to represent each element, but you may use anything that you personally associate with the element.

Air/East: sword, athame, wand, feathers, bells, ribbons, Ace of Swords Tarot.

Fire/South: candles, thorns, wands and other phallic objects, dragons, matches, masculine aspect, Ace of Wands Tarot.

Water/West: chalice, cup, seashells, crystal ball, ankh, mirror, water/wine, feminine aspect, Ace of Cups Tarot.

Earth/North: pentacle, altar, metals, coins, flowers/herbs, soil, sand, salt, nuts and seeds, Ace of Pentacles Tarot.

Elemental Circle Casting Ritual

Prepare the area in which you wish to cast your circle, you can place objects representing the elements at their corresponding cardinal direction.

With your wand or other tool in your dominant hand point towards the east side of the circle and say the following:

"I call upon the Guardian of the East, Element of Air, to watch over this sacred space."

Envision the Guardian appearing in the east, bow to acknowledge the Guardian, and turn to the south. With your hand extended say the following:

"I call upon the Guardian of the South, Element of Fire, to watch over this sacred space."

Envision the Guardian, bow to acknowledge him, and turn to the west. With your hand extended say the following:

"I call upon the Guardian of the West, Element of Water, to watch over this sacred space."

As you envision the arrival of the Guardian, bow in respect, and turn to the north. With your arm still extended, say the following:

"I call upon the Guardian of the North, Element of Earth, to watch over this sacred space."

9

Raise your hand up into the air and say the following:

"I call upon the spirit to protect this space, as I will, the circle is cast."

After you are done conducting your ritual simply wave your hand or athame through the circle with the intention of closing it.

Joyful Heart Cleansing

In this ritual, we invite the spirit of Aphrodite, the goddess of love and beauty, to cleanse and uplift our hearts. Aphrodite's presence brings forth a gentle reminder of the power of love, self-acceptance, and joy.

Ritual Items:

Rose quartz crystal

Pink candle

Jasmine incense

A small bowl of rose petals

Light the pink candle and the jasmine incense, allowing their fragrances to fill the air with a soothing ambiance.

Hold the rose quartz crystal in your hands and take a few deep breaths, allowing yourself to relax and become present in the moment. Feel the loving energy of the crystal as it radiates warmth and compassion.

Close your eyes and visualize a soft pink light surrounding your heart. See this light expanding and filling your entire body, infusing every cell with love, happiness, and harmony. Embrace the joy that flows within you.

Take a handful of rose petals from the bowl and scatter them around you in a clockwise direction. As you do so, affirm aloud or in your mind:

"With each petal, I release any sadness, pain, or negativity from my heart.
I welcome the joy, love, and light that reside within me."

Hold the rose quartz crystal to your heart and speak the following words:

"Beloved Aphrodite, goddess of love and beauty,
I invite your presence and guidance in this moment.
May you bless and cleanse my heart,
Filling it with love, happiness, and joy.
As I release the old, I make space for new beginnings.
Thank you, Aphrodite, for your divine grace."

Sit in stillness for a few moments, allowing the energy to integrate within you. Visualize your heart bathed in a vibrant pink light, filled with love and radiance.

When you are ready, extinguish the candle and let the incense burn out naturally. Collect the rose petals and return them to nature, releasing any remaining attachments or burdens.

Remember that the power of love resides within you. By engaging in this ritual, you honor your heart, invite joy into your life, and awaken the beautiful essence that defines you. May your heart be forever blessed with the magic of love and the embrace of Aphrodite's gentle presence.

Embracing Inner Beauty

In this ritual, we call upon the energy of Freya, the Norse goddess of beauty and fertility. Freya's essence inspires us to embrace our unique beauty, both inside and out, and to celebrate the radiance that flows from within.

Ritual Items:

Hand mirror

Pink lipstick

Rosewater spray

Find a quiet and comfortable space where you can focus on yourself and your reflection without interruptions. Place the hand mirror in front of you, ensuring that you can see your face clearly.

Take a few deep breaths, allowing yourself to relax and center your energy. Feel a sense of self-acceptance and appreciation growing within you.

Gently pick up the pink lipstick and apply it to your lips while looking into the mirror. As you do so, affirm aloud or silently:

*"With this lipstick, I celebrate my unique beauty.
I embrace my authentic self and radiate confidence.
I am beautiful inside and out, and I shine with joy."*

Close your eyes for a moment and visualize a soft pink light enveloping your entire being. Feel the love and acceptance emanating from this light, embracing every aspect of who you are.

Open your eyes and pick up the rosewater spray. Mist it lightly over your body, feeling its gentle touch refreshing and revitalizing your skin. As you do this, recite the following words:

*"Freya, goddess of beauty and fertility,
I invite your presence and blessings in this sacred space.
May your grace and radiance infuse my being,
Awakening my inner beauty and confidence.
Thank you, Freya, for embracing me in your loving embrace."*

Hold the hand mirror and gaze into your own eyes. Say the following:

"I am beautiful just as I am. My beauty shines from within.

I honor and love myself completely."

Spend a few moments admiring your reflection, appreciating the unique features that make you who you are. Embrace the beauty that emanates from within and let it illuminate your surroundings.

Express gratitude to Freya for her presence and the energy she has bestowed upon you. Place the hand mirror in a special place or carry it with you as a reminder of your inherent beauty.

Through this ritual, you honor the goddess Freya and awaken your own inner radiance. Embrace your unique beauty with love, confidence, and gratitude. May you always recognize the captivating essence that resides within you and let it shine brightly for all the world to see.

Serene Sleep Spell

In this soothing ritual, we call upon the calming energy of Selene, the Greek goddess of the moon. Selene's gentle presence guides us into a peaceful slumber, ensuring restful sleep and sweet dreams.

Ritual Items:

Lavender essential oil
Small pouch filled with dried chamomile flowers
White candle

Create a serene and cozy environment in your bedroom. Dim the lights (or turn them off) and ensure that you won't be disturbed during this ritual. Place the white candle on a safe surface and light it, allowing its soft glow to fill the room.

Take a moment to center yourself and relax. Inhale the soothing aroma of the lavender essential oil, letting its fragrance wash over you. Take a few deep breaths, releasing any tension or worries.

Whisper or think the following words:

"Selene, goddess of the moon,
I invite your divine, serene presence.
Wrap me in your soothing embrace,
And guide me into a restful slumber.
May my dreams be filled with tranquility and joy."

Take the pouch filled with dried chamomile flowers and hold it in your hands. Envision it as a vessel of relaxation and comfort. Speak the following words:

"Chamomile, herb of relaxation and serenity,
I invite your gentle essence.
Fill my dreams with your calming properties,
Bringing peace and tranquility to my rest.
So mote it be."

Place the pouch under your pillow or tuck it nearby, allowing the aroma of chamomile to promote restful sleep.

Sit or lie comfortably near the lit white candle. Gaze into the flame and let your mind drift before blowing out the candle. Visualize a serene moonlit landscape, feeling Selene's energy embracing you. Surrender to the peaceful ambiance and let yourself drift off into a deep and restorative sleep.

May this ritual invite Selene's tranquil energy into your nights, bringing you restful sleep and dreams filled with peace and beauty. Embrace the soothing power of this ritual and wake up refreshed, ready to embrace the new day with a heart full of tranquility.

Yoruba Waters of Love

In this ritual we invoke the healing energies of the element of water and call upon the compassionate presence of Yemaya, the Yoruba goddess of the ocean. Yemaya's nurturing embrace brings forth emotional healing and restores a sense of inner peace.

Ritual Items:

Small bowl or basin of purified water
Pink or blue flower petals
Sea salt
Rose quartz crystal

Place the bowl in front of you and take a few deep breaths to center yourself. Sprinkle a pinch of sea salt into the water, symbolizing the purification and cleansing of emotional wounds. Stir gently with your finger, allowing the salt to dissolve completely.

Hold the rose quartz crystal in your hands, feeling its gentle energy radiating through your palms. Close your eyes and visualize a serene ocean scene, with waves gently lapping at the shore. Feel the soothing presence of Yemaya surrounding you.

Open your eyes and drop the flower petals into the water, one by one. As each petal touches the water's surface, visualize it carrying away any emotional pain or sorrow. Speak the following words:

"Yemaya, goddess of the ocean's embrace,
I call upon your healing waters of love.
Wash away my emotional wounds and bring me solace.
Let the tides of your compassion restore my inner peace.
With gratitude, I honor your nurturing presence."

Dip your fingers into the water and sprinkle a few droplets over your face, as if washing away any traces of emotional distress. Feel the soothing touch of the water, knowing that it carries the blessings of Yemaya's healing energy.

Gently place the rose quartz crystal into the water, allowing it to infuse with the healing properties of the element. Let it rest there for a few moments, absorbing the energy of the ritual.

Take a moment to reflect on any emotions or burdens you wish to release. Allow yourself to feel the weight lifting from your heart as Yemaya's loving energy permeates your being.

Express gratitude to Yemaya for her presence and healing. Pour the water outside, returning it to the Earth with reverence and gratitude.

By immersing yourself in the healing waters of Yemaya, you open the pathway to emotional restoration and inner peace. Embrace her compassionate embrace and let her healing touch wash away any emotional burdens. May you find solace and renewed strength as you journey on the path of healing and self-discovery.

Blossoming Confidence

In this ritual we invoke the energy of Lakshmi, the Hindu goddess of abundance and beauty. Lakshmi's radiant presence inspires us to embrace our inner confidence and cultivate a sense of self-assuredness.

Ritual Items:

Small mirror
Pink or yellow candle
Jasmine incense
A flower of your choice

Find a quiet and comfortable space where you can focus on yourself and your reflection. Set up the small mirror, candle, and incense in front of you.

Light the pink or yellow candle, symbolizing the illumination of your confidence and inner radiance. Light the jasmine incense, allowing its fragrance to permeate the air with a sense of grace and beauty.

Take a few deep breaths, grounding yourself in the present moment. Gaze into the mirror and look deeply into your reflection, connecting with your inner self.

Say the following:

"I am confident, worthy, and deserving of all the blessings that come my way.
My beauty shines from within, and I embrace my unique qualities.
With the support of Lakshmi's abundant energy, I step into my own power."

Take the flower in your hands and hold it close to your heart. Feel its energy merging with yours, infusing you with confidence and self-assurance.

Place the flower in front of the mirror, allowing its beauty to reflect back at you. As you admire the flower's petals, envision your own confidence blossoming and unfolding, just like the flower.

Take a moment to visualize yourself engaging in activities or situations that require confidence. See yourself radiating with self-assuredness and grace, knowing that you have the support of Lakshmi's abundant energy.

Express gratitude to Lakshmi for her presence and the confidence she instills within you. Allow the candle and incense to burn out naturally, symbolizing the continuous illumination of your confidence.

Through this ritual, you honor the goddess Lakshmi and awaken your own inner confidence. Embrace your unique qualities, knowing that you are deserving of abundance and beauty. May your confidence blossom like a radiant flower, illuminating your path with self-assuredness and empowerment.

Bonds of Friendship

In this ritual, we invite the joyful energy of Hestia, the Greek goddess of hearth and home, to bless and strengthen the bonds of friendship. Hestia's presence encourages warmth, harmony, and deep connections among friends.

Ritual Items:

Pink or red yarn

Small charm or token representing friendship (e.g., heart-shaped pendant)

Candle (color of your choice)

Small bowl of dried herbs or flowers (such as lavender or rose petals)

Gather your friends in a comfortable and welcoming space. Light the candle at the center, creating a warm and inviting atmosphere.

Each person takes a piece of the pink or red yarn, representing the thread that binds their friendship. Hold the yarn in your hands and visualize the bond of friendship growing stronger and more vibrant.

Pass the charm or token representing friendship around the circle. As each person holds the charm, they can share a heartfelt message or wish for the group, affirming the value and love shared in their friendship.

Once the charm has made its way around the circle, gather the ends of the yarn together, symbolizing the unity and connection of the group. Tie a secure knot, infusing it with the intention of a strong and lasting friendship.

Lightly dip the yarn knot into the small bowl of dried herbs or flowers, allowing it to be coated with the essence and blessings of friendship. Each person can take turns gently touching the yarn to their heart, infusing it with their own love and positive energy.

Together, hold the knotted yarn in front of the lit candle, basking in the warm glow. Repeat the following words together or take turns saying them:

"Hestia, goddess of hearth and home,
We call upon your presence and blessings.
May the bond of our friendship be forever strong,
Filled with warmth, laughter, and love.

Place the knotted yarn in a safe place, such as an altar or a special box dedicated to friendship. Whenever you gather with your friends, you can reflect on this ritual and the magical bond you share.

Allow the candle to burn out naturally, symbolizing the lasting flame of friendship and the warmth it brings to your lives.

Through this ritual, you celebrate and strengthen the bonds of friendship, honoring the presence of Hestia. May your friendship be infused with love, laughter, and shared memories, creating a sacred space where all hearts find solace and joy.

Faerie's Slumber

In this enchanting ritual, we invite the ethereal energy of the Moonlit Faeries to guide us into a night of restful sleep and enchanting dreams. These feminine beings offer us the opportunity to explore the realms of imagination, intuition, and magic.

Ritual Items:

Lavender essential oil

Small fabric or organza bag

Dream journal or notebook

White candle

Find a peaceful and comfortable space where you can relax before bedtime. Light the white candle, creating a soft and calming ambiance in the room.

Take a moment to inhale the soothing aroma of lavender essential oil, allowing its calming fragrance to wash over you. Rub a few drops of the oil on your temples and wrists, inviting tranquility and preparing your senses for a peaceful night's sleep.

Hold the small fabric or organza bag in your hands. Visualize it as a vessel that will hold your dreams, keeping them safe and vibrant. Whisper or think the following words:

"Moonlit Faeries, enchantresses of dreams, I invite your ethereal presence this night.

Guide me into the realm of dreams with your delicate touch.

May my dreams be vivid, inspiring, and filled with mystical wonders.

I embrace the mysteries that await in the realm of sleep."

Place the dream journal or notebook beside the candle. As you prepare to sleep, keep it nearby to record any dreams or insights that may come to you during the night.

Sit or lie comfortably near the lit candle. Gaze into the flame, allowing its flickering light to capture your attention. Close your eyes and take several deep breaths, focusing your intention on a night of restful sleep and enchanting dreams.

When you feel ready, blow out the candle, symbolizing the transition from wakefulness to the realm of dreams. Whisper the following affirmation or repeat it in your mind:

"As the candle flame extinguishes, I enter the world of dreams.
Moonlit Faeries, guide me on a magical journey of wonder and insight.
I trust in the wisdom and enchantment that unfold in the realm of sleep."

Slip the small fabric or organza bag under your pillow or place it beside you on your nightstand, imagining it as a conduit to capture the essence of your dreams.

In the morning, upon awakening, reach for your dream journal or notebook and record any dreams, symbols, or insights that you remember. Reflect on these messages from your subconscious and honor the guidance that they offer.

Through this sweet dreams enchantment, you invite the presence of the Moonlit Faeries to bless your sleep and journey into the world of dreams. May your nights be filled with restful slumber and dreams that inspire, enlighten, and awaken your inner magic.

Aphrodite's Ritual of Self Love

In this empowering ritual, we call upon the energy of Aphrodite, the Greek goddess of love and beauty. Aphrodite's radiant presence inspires us to embrace the essence of self-love and honor our intrinsic worth.

Ritual Items:

Hand mirror
Pink or rose-colored candle
Rose quartz crystal
A small bouquet of pink flowers

Find a quiet and sacred space where you can focus on yourself and your reflection. Set up the hand mirror, candle, rose quartz crystal, and bouquet of pink flowers in front of you.

Light the pink or rose-colored candle, symbolizing the illumination of self-love and inner beauty. Let its gentle glow fill the room with warmth and tenderness.

Hold the rose quartz crystal in your hands, allowing its loving energy to radiate through your palms. Close your eyes and take a few deep breaths, grounding yourself in the present moment.

Gently open your eyes and gaze into the hand mirror. Meet your own eyes in the reflection and affirm the following words:

"I am worthy of love and acceptance.
My beauty emanates from within, shining brightly.
I honor myself with compassion and kindness.
I am deserving of all the love and joy that life offers."

Hold the bouquet of pink flowers in your hands, feeling their delicate petals and the energy of their vibrant color. Visualize the blossoming of self-love within you, just like the flowers opening to reveal their beauty.

Place the bouquet beside the mirror, symbolizing the harmony between your inner and outer beauty. Allow the mirror to reflect the radiance of the flowers, reinforcing your own inherent loveliness.

Take the rose quartz crystal and gently touch it to your heart. Feel its loving vibrations infusing your being with self-acceptance and compassion. Say the following:

"Aphrodite, goddess of love and beauty,
I invoke your presence and blessings in this sacred space.
May your grace and confidence inspire my own self-love.
With gratitude, I embrace my unique beauty and worth."

Take a few moments to bask in the loving energy and affirmations of self-love. Embrace the feelings of worthiness and acceptance that arise within you.

When you are ready, express gratitude to Aphrodite for her presence and the empowerment she has bestowed upon you. Allow the candle to burn out naturally, symbolizing the continuous flame of self-love in your life.

Through this ritual of self-love, you honor the goddess Aphrodite and awaken your own inner beauty. Embrace your unique qualities, knowing that you are deserving of love and acceptance. May your journey be filled with self-love and the confidence to shine your authentic light into the world.

Inner Goddess Empowerment

In this empowering ritual, we connect with the energy of Artemis, the Greek goddess of the hunt and the moon. Artemis' fierce independence and connection to nature inspire us to tap into our own inner strength and embrace our inner goddess.

Ritual Items:

Green or silver candle

Moonstone crystal

A small bouquet of fresh herbs, such as lavender, rosemary, and sage

A piece of paper and a pen

Find a serene outdoor space or create a sacred space indoors where you can connect with nature. Set up the green or silver candle, moonstone crystal, bouquet of fresh herbs, and the piece of paper and pen.

Light the green or silver candle, symbolizing the awakening of your inner goddess and connection to nature. Allow its gentle flame to illuminate the space and bring a sense of empowerment.

Hold the moonstone crystal in your hands, feeling its cool and soothing energy. Close your eyes and visualize the ethereal glow of the moon bathing you in its light. Invoke the presence of Artemis and her fierce independence.

Open your eyes and take the piece of paper and pen. Write down qualities and strengths that you associate with your inner goddess. Reflect on the aspects of yourself that make you feel empowered, strong, and confident.

Take the bouquet of fresh herbs and hold it in your hands. Inhale deeply, allowing the aroma of the herbs to awaken your senses and connect you with the natural world. Feel the vitality and life force they embody.

Place the piece of paper with your affirmations under the bouquet of fresh herbs. Envision the energy of Artemis infusing the herbs and empowering the qualities you have written down.

Hold the bouquet of herbs close to your heart, feeling the energy of the goddess flowing through you.

Speak the following words:

"Artemis, goddess of the hunt and the moon,
I embrace your independent and fierce spirit.
I call upon your strength and empowerment.
Infuse me with the qualities of my inner goddess.
May I walk with confidence and grace, connected
to nature and my true self."

Spend a few moments basking in the energy of Artemis and the qualities of your inner goddess. Allow her strength and independence to fill you, empowering your mind, body, and spirit.

When you feel ready, express gratitude to Artemis for her presence and the embodiment of your inner goddess. Allow the candle to burn out naturally, symbolizing the eternal flame of empowerment within you.

Through this ritual you honor the goddess Artemis and awaken your own strength and independence. Embrace the qualities of your inner goddess, knowing that you possess the power to pursue your dreams and walk with confidence. May you embody the spirit of Artemis, connecting with nature and embracing your authentic self.

Brigid's Healing Bath

In this ritual, we invoke the nurturing energy of Brigid, the Celtic goddess of hearth, healing, and inspiration. Brigid's loving presence encourages us to prioritize self-care and embrace practices that nourish our mind, body, and spirit.

Ritual Items:

A warm and cozy blanket

Scented bath salts or essential oils (such as lavender or rose)

Herbal tea of your choice

Journal and pen

Create a peaceful and comfortable space where you can fully relax and indulge in self-care. Prepare a cozy area with cushions and soft lighting.

Wrap yourself in the warm and cozy blanket, symbolizing the embrace of Brigid's loving energy. Take a few deep breaths, allowing yourself to settle into a state of relaxation.

Prepare a warm bath infused with scented bath salts or a few drops of essential oil. As you pour the salts or oil into the water, visualize them carrying away any tension or stress, leaving you feeling renewed and rejuvenated.

Slowly immerse yourself into the warm water, feeling its soothing embrace envelop your body. Close your eyes and imagine Brigid's gentle presence surrounding you, radiating healing energy.

Sip on a cup of herbal tea, allowing its warmth to spread through you. With each sip, imagine the tea nourishing your body and providing comfort to your soul. Feel the herbal infusion infusing you with vitality and tranquility.

Take your journal and pen and allow your thoughts and feelings to flow onto the pages. Write down any reflections, aspirations, or affirmations that come to mind. Use this space to honor your journey and express gratitude for the blessings in your life.

As you relax in the bath, recite the following affirmation or create your own, speaking it with love and intention:

"Brigid, goddess of hearth and healing,

I invite your nurturing energy into this sacred self-care ritual.

May your warmth and love embrace every aspect of my being.

I honor myself with gentle care and compassion.

I am deserving of nourishment and rejuvenation.

Thank you, Brigid, for your guiding presence."

After soaking in the bath, slowly emerge from the water, feeling renewed and refreshed. Wrap yourself again in the warm blanket, allowing its comforting energy to continue enveloping you.

Spend a few moments sitting or lying in quiet reflection. Embrace the sense of tranquility and self-love that surrounds you. Bask in the gentle energy of Brigid, knowing that you have honored yourself and received her healing touch.

When you are ready, express gratitude to Brigid for her presence and the self-care you have nurtured. Set aside your journal, blow out any candles, and slowly transition back into your daily routine, carrying the essence of this self-care ritual with you.

Through this ritual you honor the goddess Brigid and nourish your mind, body, and spirit.

Embrace practices that prioritize your well-being, knowing that you are deserving of love, healing, and rejuvenation. May you continue to nurture yourself and find solace in the gentle embrace of Brigid's nurturing energy.

Abundance and Prosperity

In this ritual we invoke the abundant energy of Lakshmi, the Hindu goddess of wealth, prosperity, and abundance. Lakshmi's presence brings forth blessings and opportunities for financial and material abundance, as well as spiritual fulfillment.

Ritual Items:

Green candle

Citrine crystal

A small bowl of rice or grains

A piece of paper and a pen

Find a quiet and dedicated space where you can focus on the energy of abundance. Set up the green candle, citrine crystal, small bowl of rice or grains, and the piece of paper and pen.

Light the green candle, symbolizing the growth and manifestation of abundance in your life. Allow its warm glow to fill the space and create an atmosphere of prosperity.

Take the citrine crystal in your hands, feeling its vibrant energy and connection to abundance. Close

43

your eyes and envision golden light surrounding you, symbolizing the blessings of Lakshmi's abundant energy.

Open your eyes and place the piece of paper and pen in front of you. Write down your intentions for abundance and prosperity. Be specific and heartfelt, expressing your desires and goals in a positive and affirmative manner.

Hold the bowl of rice or grains in your hands. Feel their symbolism of nourishment, sustenance, and abundance. Visualize the grains as seeds of prosperity, ready to be planted and grow in your life.

Place the piece of paper with your intentions under the bowl of rice or grains, allowing the energy of Lakshmi to infuse your desires with her blessings. See your intentions being nurtured and supported.

Hold the citrine crystal and say the following invocation:

"Lakshmi, goddess of wealth and abundance,
I invite your blessings and prosperity into my life.
May your golden energy illuminate my path to success.
As I plant the seeds of my intentions,
I trust in your guidance and infinite abundance.
With gratitude, I open myself to receive your blessings."

Gently pour the rice or grains from the bowl onto the piece of paper with your intentions, symbolizing the nurturing and growth of your desires. Feel the energy of Lakshmi blessing and amplifying your intentions.

Keep the piece of paper with your intentions and the citrine crystal in a sacred space, such as an altar or a prosperity corner in your home. Whenever you see them, be reminded of your intentions and the abundance that is flowing into your life.

Express gratitude to Lakshmi for her presence and the blessings she brings. Allow the candle to burn out naturally, symbolizing the continuous flame of abundance and prosperity in your life.

Activating Inner Strength

In this empowering ritual, we call upon the energy of Durga, the Hindu goddess of strength and protection. Durga's fierce and courageous presence inspires us to tap into our inner power and overcome challenges with confidence and resilience.

Ritual Items:

Red or orange candle
Tiger's eye crystal
A small piece of paper and a pen
A small bowl of salt

Find a quiet and dedicated space where you can focus on harnessing your inner strength. Set up the red or orange candle, tiger's eye crystal, small piece of paper and pen, and the small bowl of salt.

Light the red or orange candle, symbolizing the fiery strength and determination within you. Allow its warm glow to create an atmosphere of empowerment and courage.

Hold the tiger's eye crystal in your hands, feeling its grounding energy and connection to personal power. Close your eyes and envision a radiant light surrounding you, representing Durga's protective embrace and the strength she bestows.

Open your eyes and take the piece of paper and pen. Write down any challenges, fears, or obstacles that you wish to overcome. Be honest and specific, expressing your intentions to conquer and rise above them.

Hold the small bowl of salt in your hands. Feel its purifying and protective energy. Visualize the salt as a cleansing force, removing any negativity or self-doubt that may hinder your inner strength.

Place the piece of paper with your challenges and intentions under the bowl of salt, allowing the energy of Durga to infuse your desires with her transformative power. See your challenges being dissolved and replaced with strength and resilience.

Hold the tiger's eye crystal and say the following:

*"Durga, goddess of strength and protection,
I invoke your power to awaken my inner strength.*

Gently pour a small amount of salt onto the piece of paper, symbolizing the transformative energy of Durga infusing your challenges with strength and protection. Feel the salt purifying and fortifying your intentions.

Keep the piece of paper with your challenges and the tiger's eye crystal in a sacred space, such as an altar or a personal power corner. Whenever you see them, be reminded of your inner strength and the protection that surrounds you.

Express gratitude to Durga for her presence and the empowering energy she brings. Allow the candle to burn out naturally, symbolizing the continuous flame of inner strength and courage in your life.

Through this ritual of embracing inner strength, you honor the goddess Durga and awaken your own innate power. Embrace your challenges with courage and resilience, knowing that you have the strength within you to overcome them. May you stand tall in the face of adversity and emerge victorious, embodying the fierce and courageous spirit of Durga.

Quan Yin's Healing Heart Ritual

In this soothing ritual, we connect with the compassionate energy of Quan Yin, the Chinese goddess of mercy and healing. Quan Yin's gentle presence brings comfort and emotional healing, allowing us to release pain and find solace within our hearts.

Ritual Items:

Pink or white candle

Rose quartz crystal

A comfortable cushion or chair

Soft instrumental music or nature sounds

Find a quiet and serene space where you can sit comfortably. Set up the pink or white candle, rose quartz crystal, cushion or chair, and prepare the instrumental music or nature sounds.

Light the pink or white candle, symbolizing the healing light of Quan Yin's compassion. Allow its soft glow to create a serene ambiance, inviting comfort and emotional healing.

Hold the rose quartz crystal in your hands, feeling its gentle and loving energy. Close your eyes and take a few deep breaths, allowing yourself to relax and let go of any tension.

Place the rose quartz crystal on your heart center, located in the middle of your chest. Feel its soothing vibrations spreading warmth and love throughout your heart space.

Begin playing the music or nature sounds. Let the calming melodies or natural sounds envelop you, creating a peaceful and harmonious atmosphere.

Take a moment to focus on your breath. Inhale deeply, imagining you are inhaling healing light, and exhale slowly, releasing any emotional pain or burdens from your heart.

With each inhale, visualize the pink light of Quan Yin's compassion entering your heart, bringing comfort and healing. With each exhale, imagine any pain or sadness being released, making space for love and healing to flow.

As you continue to breathe deeply, repeat the following:

"Quan Yin, goddess of mercy and healing,
I invite your compassionate energy into my heart.
Release any pain or sorrow that resides within,
And fill my heart with love, comfort, and healing.
I am worthy of emotional well-being and serenity."

Sit in this healing space for as long as you feel comfortable, allowing the energy of Quan Yin and the rose quartz crystal to work their magic on your heart. Feel the emotional burdens lifting and the love flowing freely within.

When you are ready, express gratitude to Quan Yin for her presence and the healing she has bestowed upon your heart. Gently blow out the candle, symbolizing the transformation and release of emotional pain.

Through this healing heart meditation, you honor the goddess Quan Yin and invite her compassionate energy to heal and comfort your heart. Embrace the process of emotional healing, knowing that you are deserving of love, solace, and serenity. May your heart be filled with the gentle light of Quan Yin's compassion and find deep healing in this sacred space.

Moonlit Manifestations of Selene

In this ritual, we connect with the mystical energy of Selene, the Greek goddess of the moon. Selene's ethereal presence illuminates the path of manifestation and empowers us to bring our desires into reality under the moon's gentle glow.

Ritual Items:

Silver or white candle

Moonstone crystal

Pen and paper

A small pouch or envelope

Find a tranquil outdoor space or a cozy spot near a window where you can witness the moon's luminosity. Set up the silver or white candle, moonstone crystal, pen and paper, and the small pouch or envelope.

Light the silver or white candle, symbolizing the moon's radiant energy and its connection to the manifestation of dreams. Allow its soft glow to create a serene ambiance, inviting the moon's guidance.

Hold the moonstone crystal in your hands, feeling its calming energy and connection to the moon's cycles. Close your eyes and imagine the moonlight enveloping you, filling you with its mystical power.

Open your eyes and take the pen and paper. Write down your deepest desires and intentions, being specific and heartfelt. Let your words flow with clarity and conviction, as if you are declaring them to the moon.

Hold the moonstone crystal against your heart, infusing it with your intentions and desires. Visualize the moon's light blessing your desires and activating their manifestation.

Place the paper with your intentions and desires into the small pouch or envelope, symbolizing the containment of your dreams.

Hold it in your hands and speak or think the following words:

"Selene, goddess of the moon and manifestation,
I call upon your ethereal energy to guide my intentions.
Under your luminous glow, I declare my desires to the universe.
May the moonlight infuse my dreams with divine energy.
With gratitude, I trust in the power of manifestation."

Hold the pouch or envelope close to the candle flame, allowing its warmth to seal the energy of your intentions. Imagine the flame activating the manifestation process, infusing your desires with cosmic energy.

Place the pouch or envelope in a sacred space, such as an altar or a special drawer dedicated to manifestation. Each night, hold it in your hands and visualize your desires coming to fruition, connecting with the energy of Selene.

Express gratitude to Selene for her presence and the guidance she provides on your manifestation journey. Allow the candle to burn out

55

naturally, symbolizing the continuous connection between you and the moon's energy.

Through this manifestation ritual, you honor the goddess Selene and tap into the power of the moon to manifest your desires. Embrace the energy of the moon, knowing that you have the ability to create and manifest your dreams. May the gentle glow of Selene's light illuminate your path of manifestation and bring your desires into reality.

Yoruba Energy Cleanse

In this purifying ritual, we invoke the harmonizing energy of Oshun, the Yoruba goddess of love, beauty, and harmony. Oshun's radiant presence brings balance and positivity, cleansing our energetic space and promoting inner harmony.

Ritual Items:

sage bundle or palo santo stick

A small bowl of water

Honey or a sweet-smelling flower

Feather or fan

Find a quiet and sacred space where you can focus on cleansing and harmonizing your energy. Set up the white sage bundle or palo santo stick, the small bowl of water, honey or flower, and the feather or fan.

Light the sage or palo santo, allowing the smoke to fill the space. As the smoke rises, visualize it purifying and cleansing the energy around you, removing any negativity or stagnant vibrations.

Dip your fingers into the small bowl of water and gently sprinkle a few droplets around the room, symbolizing the purification of the space. As you do this, affirm your intention for harmony and balance.

Take the honey or sweet-smelling flower and hold it in your hands. Feel its energy and connection to Oshun's loving and harmonizing essence. Set the intention for sweetness and positivity to flow into your life.

Use the feather or fan to gently waft the smoke from the sage bundle or palo santo stick around your body, focusing on each energy center (chakra) from the crown of your head to the soles of your feet. Visualize any stagnant or negative energy being released and replaced with harmonious and positive vibrations.

As you fan the smoke, recite the following affirmation or create your own, speaking it with intention and love:

"Oshun, goddess of love and harmony,
I invite your presence to cleanse and balance my
energy.
Release any negativity or disharmony within me,

And fill me with your loving and harmonious essence.

May my energy be aligned and vibrating with positivity."

Place the honey or sweet-smelling flower on your altar or in a special place, symbolizing the sweetness and positivity you have invited into your life. Feel the energy of Oshun's loving embrace surrounding you.

Take a moment to sit in quiet reflection, basking in the harmonious energy that surrounds you. Feel the balance and positivity permeating every aspect of your being.

Express gratitude to Oshun for her presence and the cleansing of your energy. Allow the incense to burn out naturally, symbolizing the completion of the harmonizing energy cleanse.

Through this ritualistic cleansing, you honor the goddess Oshun and invite her loving and harmonious energy into your life. Embrace the purification and balance of your energy, knowing that you deserve to vibrate with positivity and harmony. May Oshun's presence guide you toward a life filled with love, beauty, and inner harmony.

Creative Inspiration Ritual

In this spell of creative inspiration, we connect with the vibrant energy of Saraswati, the Hindu goddess of knowledge, arts, and creativity. Saraswati's divine presence stimulates our creative flow and empowers us to express our unique gifts and talents.

Ritual Items:

Yellow candle

Clear quartz crystal

A blank canvas or sketchbook

Art supplies of your choice (paints, pencils, markers, etc.)

Find a quiet and inspiring space where you can tap into your creativity. Set up the yellow candle, clear quartz crystal, blank canvas or sketchbook, and your chosen art supplies.

Light the yellow candle, symbolizing the spark of inspiration and the radiance of Saraswati's creative energy. Allow its warm glow to infuse the space with a vibrant and uplifting atmosphere.

Hold the clear quartz crystal in your hands, feeling its clarity and amplifying properties. Close your eyes and imagine a stream of creative energy flowing into you, connecting you with Saraswati's inspiration.

Open your eyes and place the crystal beside the candle, symbolizing its connection to the divine source of inspiration. Set the intention to tap into your creative flow and express yourself authentically.

Take the blank canvas or sketchbook and your art supplies. Close your eyes and take a few deep breaths, centering yourself in the present moment. Visualize the creative energy filling your being.

When you feel ready, open your eyes and begin creating. Allow your intuition to guide your hand, expressing yourself freely on the canvas or sketchbook. Let go of any judgments or expectations, embracing the process of creation.

As you create, say the following affirmation, or create your own, speaking it with passion and purpose:

"Saraswati, goddess of knowledge and creativity,

Let the creative energy guide you as you paint, draw, or express yourself through art. Allow yourself to fully immerse in the process, connecting with the divine inspiration that flows through you.

When you feel complete, take a moment to appreciate your creation. Acknowledge the unique expression of your inner self and the connection you have established with Saraswati's creative energy.

Express gratitude to Saraswati for her presence and the inspiration she has bestowed upon you. Allow the candle to burn out naturally, symbolizing the continuous flame of creative inspiration in your life.

Through this ritual you honor the goddess Saraswati and invoke her divine energy to flow through your artistic expression. Embrace your creative power, knowing that you are a vessel for divine inspiration. May Saraswati's presence guide you on a journey of self-expression, unleashing your unique gifts and talents for the world to see.

Blooming Confidence

Blooming Confidence Ritual

In this ritual we'll be calling upon the energy of Freya, the Norse goddess of love, beauty, and fertility. Freya's radiant presence empowers us to embrace our authentic selves and cultivate unwavering confidence, allowing our true essence to blossom.

Ritual Items:

Pink or red candle

Sunstone crystal

A small mirror

Fresh flowers of your choice

Conducting the Ritual:

Find a quiet and sacred space where you can focus on cultivating confidence. Set up the pink or red candle, sunstone crystal, small mirror, and arrange the fresh flowers in a vase or small bouquet.

Light the pink or red candle, symbolizing the flame of confidence and self-love. Let its warm glow fill the space, creating an atmosphere of empowerment and authenticity.

Hold the sunstone crystal in your hands, feeling its energizing and uplifting energy. Close your eyes and envision yourself radiating with confidence, embracing your unique beauty and inner power.

Open your eyes and gaze into the small mirror. Meet your own eyes in the reflection and affirm the following words:

"Freya, goddess of love and beauty,
I invoke your empowering energy in this sacred ritual.
Reflecting upon my true essence, I embrace my beauty and worth.
With unwavering confidence, I allow my true self to blossom.
I am deserving of love, success, and happiness."

Place the mirror in front of the lit candle, allowing its flame to reflect upon your reflection. Visualize the flame infusing your image with confidence, amplifying your inner radiance.

Take the fresh flowers in your hands, feeling their vibrant energy and connection to growth and blooming. Hold them close to your heart, envisioning your confidence and self-love blossoming like the flowers.

Speak the following as you hold the flowers:

"Freya, goddess of fertility and empowerment,
I invite your energy to awaken my blooming confidence.
Like these flowers, I allow my true self to flourish.
With gratitude, I embrace my authentic beauty and power."

Arrange the fresh flowers in a prominent place, such as your altar or a spot that you frequent. Let them serve as a reminder of your blooming confidence and inner strength.

Take a few moments to bask in the energy of empowerment and authenticity. Embrace the feeling of confidence radiating from within you, knowing that you are worthy and capable.

Express gratitude to Freya for her presence and the empowerment she has bestowed upon you. Allow the candle to burn out naturally, symbolizing the continuous flame of confidence and self-love in your life.

Through this blooming confidence ritual, you honor the goddess Freya and awaken your own inner power and beauty. Embrace your authentic self, knowing that you possess unwavering confidence and deserve to shine. May your confidence bloom like the flowers, radiating your unique essence and attracting love, success, and happiness into your life.

Hecate's Liminal Dreamcraft

In this ritual we connect with the mystical energy of Hecate, the Greek liminal goddess of magic, crossroads, and the moon. Hecate's ethereal presence allows us to delve into the realm of dreams, seeking wisdom, inspiration, and guidance from the depths of our subconscious mind.

Ritual Items:

Purple candle
Amethyst crystal
Dream journal or notebook
Comfortable sleepwear or pajamas

Find a serene and peaceful space where you can focus on your dreams. Set up the purple candle, amethyst crystal, dream journal or notebook, and wear your comfortable sleepwear or pajamas.

Light the candle to symbolize the gateway to the dream realm. Let its soft glow create an atmosphere of tranquility and invite the presence of Hecate into your space.

Hold the amethyst crystal in your hands, feeling its soothing and calming energy. Close your eyes and imagine a veil lifting, allowing you to enter the realm of dreams with Hecate as your guide.

Open your eyes and place the amethyst crystal beside the lit candle. Set the intention to connect with your dreams and receive insights, wisdom, and guidance from your subconscious mind with Hecate's guidance.

Prepare your dream journal or notebook by placing it beside the candle and crystal. Keep a pen or pencil nearby for recording your dreams upon awakening.

Before going to sleep, hold the dream journal or notebook in your hands and speak or think the following words:

"Hecate, goddess of magic and the moon,
I invite your presence into my dream realm.
Guide me through the depths of my subconscious mind.
Grant me wisdom, inspiration, and insight as I sleep.
I am open to receive and remember my dreams."

Place the dream journal or notebook under your pillow or near your bed, symbolizing your intention to remember and record your dreams upon awakening.

Wear your comfortable sleepwear or pajamas, creating a sense of relaxation and readiness for a restful night's sleep.

Just before closing your eyes to sleep, gaze at the flickering flame of the candle and affirm:

"With Hecate as my guide, I enter the realm of dreams.

My mind is open and receptive to the messages that unfold.

May my dreams be a source of wisdom, insight, and inspiration."

Blow out the candle. As you drift into sleep, trust in Hecate's presence and guidance. Upon waking in the morning, reach for your dream journal or notebook and record any dreams, impressions, or symbols that you remember.

Throughout the day, reflect on your dreams and contemplate their deeper meanings. Use the insights gained from your dreams to inform your waking life and decisions.

Express gratitude to Hecate for her presence and the wisdom revealed through your dreams. Allow the candle to burn out naturally, symbolizing the continuous connection between your conscious and subconscious realms.

Through this enchanting dream invocation with Hecate, you honor the goddess of magic and the moon. Embrace the wisdom, inspiration, and guidance that your dreams offer, knowing that they hold profound insights from your subconscious mind. May Hecate guide you on a journey of self-discovery and illuminate your path with the treasures found within your dreams.

Lunar Blessings of Chang'e

In this empowering ritual, we connect with the graceful and powerful energy of Chang'e, the Chinese goddess of the moon. Her radiant presence offers blessings and empowerment, guiding us towards inner strength and personal transformation under the full moon's luminous glow.

Ritual Items:

White or silver candle

Moonstone or jade crystal

A small bowl of water

A sprig of fresh jasmine or jasmine essential oil

Find a serene and open outdoor space where you can witness the full moon's radiant light. Set up the white or silver candle, moonstone or jade crystal, small bowl of water, and the sprig of fresh jasmine or jasmine essential oil.

Light the white or silver candle, symbolizing the illumination of the moon's energy. Let its warm glow create a sacred atmosphere, inviting the presence of Chang'e and the jade rabbit into your space.

Hold the moonstone or jade crystal in your hands, feeling its enchanting and empowering energy. Close your eyes and imagine moonlight enveloping you, awakening your inner strength and potential.

Open your eyes and place the crystal beside the lit candle. Set the intention to receive blessings and empowerment from Chang'e and to harness the transformative power of the full moon.

Take a few moments to center yourself, focusing on your breath. Inhale deeply, envisioning the radiant moonlight infusing you with confidence and inner power. Exhale slowly, releasing any self-doubt or limitations.

Hold the small bowl of water in your hands, feeling its purifying and cleansing energy. Visualize the moonlight shining upon the water, imbuing it with the blessings and transformative energy of the full moon.

Dip your fingers into the moonlit water and gently sprinkle a few droplets over your face and body. Allow the water to symbolically purify and bless you, awakening your personal power and potential.

Take the sprig of fresh jasmine or a few drops of jasmine essential oil and inhale its uplifting fragrance. Let the intoxicating aroma infuse your being, awakening your senses and connecting you to her empowering energy.

Sit in stillness, gazing at the lit candle and crystal. Visualize the full moon's radiant light enveloping you, filling you with strength, courage, and empowerment. Feel any doubts or limitations melting away, replaced by a deep sense of inner power.

Take a moment to reflect on your own journey of personal transformation. Speak or think the following invocation, expressing your intention to receive her blessings and empowerment:

"Chang'e, goddess of the moon and transformation,
I call upon your radiant energy on this sacred full moon night.
Bless me with your grace and empower my spirit.
Like the jade rabbit, guide me to embrace my true potential.
With gratitude, I embody strength, courage, and transformation."

Spend a few moments in quiet reflection, embracing the energy of empowerment and transformation. Allow her blessings to infuse your being and align you with your highest potential.

When you feel complete, express gratitude to Chang'e and the elements of the ritual—the candle, crystal, water, and jasmine—for their contributions to your empowerment. Allow the candle to burn out naturally, symbolizing the continuous flow of lunar blessings and personal transformation in your life.

Through this lunar blessing you honor the goddess and embrace her empowering energy. Embrace the process of personal transformation and self-empowerment under the full moon's radiant light. May you embody your inner strength, harness your potential.

Tiamat's Salt Soak for Radiant Skin

In this rejuvenating ritual for skin and spiritual renewal, we invoke the primordial energy of Tiamat, the Mesopotamian goddess of the saltwater ocean. Tiamat's potent presence guides us in purifying and revitalizing our skin, inviting us to dive into the depths of self-transformation and emerge renewed.

Ritual Items:

Blue or white candle

Salt (1 cup)

Aquamarine or black tourmaline crystal

Essential oil of your choice (such as eucalyptus, peppermint, or jasmine)

Create a sacred and serene space in your bathroom where you can focus on physical and spiritual renewal. Set up the candle, salt, crystal, and the oil.

Fill the bathtub with warm water, adding a cup of salt. Visualize the water becoming a vast saltwater ocean, infused with Tiamat's ancient energy, purifying and rejuvenating your skin.

Light candle, symbolizing the illuminating essence of Tiamat's oceanic power. Let its gentle flame create a tranquil ambiance, inviting Tiamat's presence to guide your renewal.

Place the crystal near the bathtub, representing the grounding and transformative energies of Tiamat. These crystals connect you to her primordial essence and assist in your renewal.

Add a few drops of your chosen oil to the bathwater. As you do so, set the intention to cleanse and revitalize your skin, invoking Tiamat's ancient wisdom to support your transformation and renewal.

Before entering the bath, stand in front of a mirror and gaze into your eyes. Affirm the following words or speak your own words of self-empowerment and rebirth:

"Tiamat, goddess of the saltwater ocean,
I invoke your primordial energy within me.
As I gaze into the mirror, I see my true essence.
I am powerful, resilient, and ready for
transformation.
With gratitude, I embrace and honor my body."

Step into the bath slowly, allowing the saltwater to envelop your body. Close your eyes and take a deep breath, immersing yourself in the rejuvenating embrace of the ocean, guided by Tiamat's ancient presence.

Visualize the ocean's gentle waves washing over you, purifying and renewing your skin. Feel the saltwater cleansing away any stagnant energy, impurities, or negative emotions, while Tiamat's transformative energy works within you.

As you soak in the bath, sense Tiamat's ancient wisdom permeating every cell, bringing deep renewal and restoration to your skin and spirit. Allow her power to awaken your inner strength and resilience.

Take a moment to reflect on the power of self-transformation and self-renewal. Speak or think the following invocation, expressing your intention to embrace the oceanic energy of Tiamat:

"Tiamat, goddess of the saltwater ocean,
I immerse myself in your ancient waters of renewal.
Cleanse and revitalize my skin, inviting transformation.

Remain in the bath for as long as desired, allowing the oceanic energy to wash over you, awakening your spirit and renewing your skin.

As you get out, gently pat your skin dry with a soft towel, embracing the sensation of freshness and renewal. As you do so, visualize any remaining impurities being washed away, leaving behind a vibrant and rejuvenated complexion.

Hold the crystal in your hands, feeling its grounding energy. Express gratitude to Tiamat for her presence and the gift of renewal, as you invite her energy to continue supporting your transformation beyond this ritual.

Extinguish the candle, if you used one, with a sense of gratitude and respect for the illumination it brought to the ritual. Allow the crystal and bathwater to naturally drain away, symbolizing the release of any remaining negative energies.

After the ritual, take a few moments to apply nourishing skincare products or oils to your cleansed skin. As you do so, set the intention for these products to enhance and maintain the radiant glow that Tiamat's energy has bestowed upon you.

Carry the renewed energy of Tiamat's oceanic power with you, embracing your skin's newfound vitality and beauty. Remember that just as the ocean goes through cycles of ebb and flow, so too does your journey of self-transformation and renewal.

Through this oceanic renewal bath you honor the goddess and immerse yourself in the transformative power of the saltwater ocean. Embrace the purifying and rejuvenating energy as you invite Tiamat's ancient wisdom to guide your path of self-transformation and renewal. May your skin radiate with vibrant health and your spirit be empowered by the primordial energy that flows within you.

Floral Blessings of Flora

In this ritual of inner harmony and balance, we connect with the gentle energy of Flora, the Roman goddess of flowers and spring. Flora's nurturing presence surrounds us as we immerse ourselves in the beauty and fragrance of flowers, allowing inner harmony to blossom within.

Ritual Items:

Assortment of fresh flowers (such as roses, jasmine, lavender, or any flowers of your choice)

Small bowl of water

Rose quartz crystal or a pink candle

Essential oil of your choice (such as rose, geranium, or ylang-ylang)

Create a serene and sacred space where you can connect with the essence of flowers and invite inner harmony. Arrange the assortment of fresh flowers, bowl, crystal or candle, and the essential oil.

Take a moment to ground yourself by focusing on your breath. Inhale deeply, allowing the air to fill your lungs, and exhale slowly, releasing any tension or distractions. Set the intention to immerse yourself in the beauty and energy of the flowers to find inner harmony.

Light the pink candle or place the rose quartz crystal near the arrangement of fresh flowers. These items represent the love and harmony that Flora brings, amplifying the energy of the ritual.

Fill the small bowl with water, symbolizing the element of emotional healing and purification. Infuse the water with a few drops of the essential oil of your choice, setting the intention to enhance the soothing and harmonizing properties.

Take a moment to appreciate the beauty and fragrance of the fresh flowers before you. Observe their colors, shapes, and textures, allowing yourself to be fully present in their presence. Feel the joy and serenity they evoke within you.

Select one flower from the assortment and hold it gently in your hands. Close your eyes and take a deep breath, inhaling its fragrance. Allow the essence of the flower to connect with your senses, inviting a sense of peace and tranquility into your being.

Place the flower in the small bowl of water, allowing it to float gracefully. As it rests upon the water's surface, visualize any disharmony or inner turmoil dissolving away, replaced by a deep sense of serenity and balance.

Immerse your hands in the water, feeling the gentle caress of the flower-infused liquid. Allow the healing properties of the flower and water to cleanse and harmonize your energy, washing away any emotional imbalances or disturbances.

Take a few moments to meditate, focusing on the flickering flame of the pink candle or the soothing energy of the rose quartz crystal. Visualize the inner petals of your being opening, revealing a blossoming harmony and balance.

Slowly and intentionally, dip your fingertips into the water and sprinkle the flower-infused droplets over your face and body. As you do so, envision the essence of the flowers enveloping you, imbuing your entire being with their harmonizing and uplifting energy.

Stand or sit in the presence of the flower arrangement, allowing the beauty and fragrance to surround you. Absorb their positive vibrations, feeling their energy infuse every cell of your body, creating a harmonious and balanced state of being.

Express gratitude to Flora, the flowers, the water, the candle/crystal, and the essential oil for their contributions to your inner harmony. Acknowledge the power of nature and its ability to bring balance and beauty into our lives.

As you complete this blessing, honor the goddess Flora and the healing energy of flowers. Embrace the essence of inner harmony that has blossomed within you. Carry this newfound sense of balance and tranquility with you as you navigate life's challenges. May the gentle presence of Flora and the beauty of flowers continue to guide you on your path toward lasting inner harmony and well-being.

Love Talisman

In this ritual of love and enchantment, we call upon the guidance of Aphrodite, the Greek goddess of love and beauty. With her blessings, we create a talisman that serves as a powerful symbol of love, attracting and nurturing deep connections in our lives.

85

Ritual Items:

Small piece of rose quartz or heart-shaped crystal

Red ribbon or string

Fresh rose petals

Love-infused essential oil (such as rose, jasmine, or ylang-ylang)

Find a calm and sacred space where you can focus on love and enchantment. Gather the small piece of rose quartz or heart-shaped crystal, red ribbon or string, fresh rose petals, and the love-infused essential oil.

Take a moment to center yourself, focusing on your breath. Inhale deeply, allowing the air to fill your lungs, and exhale slowly, releasing any tension or distractions. Set the intention to open your heart to love and invite Aphrodite's blessings.

Hold the rose quartz or heart-shaped crystal in your hands, feeling its gentle and loving energy. Close your eyes and visualize the crystal glowing with a soft pink light, radiating the essence of love and attraction.

Open your eyes and gently tie the red ribbon or string around the crystal, forming a loop to create a pendant. As you do so, set the intention that this talisman will magnetize love and deepen connections in your life.

Sprinkle a few fresh rose petals around the talisman, symbolizing Aphrodite's presence and her blessings upon your journey of love. Let the petals create a sacred space, infused with the essence of romance and beauty.

Take a moment to apply a few drops of the love-infused essential oil to your wrists or pulse points. Inhale its intoxicating fragrance, allowing it to awaken feelings of love and attraction within you.

Hold the talisman close to your heart, feeling its energy intertwining with your own. Reflect on the qualities and experiences you wish to attract in your relationships, whether it be romantic love, friendship, or familial connections.

Speak or think the following affirmation, infusing it with your heartfelt intention:

"Aphrodite, goddess of love and beauty,
I invite your blessings into my life.

May this talisman radiate love's enchanting energy,
Attracting deep connections and nurturing
affection.
With gratitude, I open my heart to love's embrace."

Wear the talisman around your neck or keep it close to your heart, allowing it to serve as a potent symbol of love and attraction. Carry it with you as a reminder of your intention to foster love and deepen connections.

As you go about your day, visualize the talisman emanating a soft pink glow, drawing love and affection toward you. Trust in the power of Aphrodite's blessings and the energy of the talisman to manifest meaningful and fulfilling relationships.

Whenever you feel the need to reconnect with love or deepen your bond with others, hold the talisman in your hands, allowing its energy to remind you of your intention and the presence of Aphrodite's love.

Express gratitude to Aphrodite for her guidance and blessings. Acknowledge the love and beauty that exists within you and around you, knowing that you are deserving of deep connections and affection.

Through this enchanting love talisman ritual, you honor Aphrodite and invite her blessings into your journey of love and connection. Embrace the power of the talisman to attract and nurture meaningful relationships in your life. May love's enchantment guide your path, allowing you to experience deep and fulfilling connections with others.

Remember that the true power of the love talisman lies within you. It serves as a physical reminder of your intention and a symbol of the love and attraction that already exists within your heart. Trust in your own innate ability to attract and cultivate love in your life.

As you embark on this journey, keep your heart open, and be receptive to the opportunities that come your way. Cherish the connections you make, and nurture them with kindness, compassion, and understanding. Know that love is a beautiful and transformative force that has the power to bring joy and fulfillment to your life.

May the enchanting energy of Aphrodite and the love talisman guide you on a path of love, deep connections, and personal growth. Embrace the magic of love and allow it to weave its spell in every aspect of your life.

Athena's Mirror

In this empowering ritual, we harness the reflective power of mirrors to cultivate self-confidence and positive self-image. Through the guidance of Athena, the Greek goddess of wisdom and courage, we affirm our inner strength and embrace our true beauty.

Ritual Items:

Handheld mirror

Pen or marker

Small notepad or sticky notes

White candle or a yellow candle

Find a quiet and comfortable space where you can focus on self-empowerment. Gather the handheld mirror, pen or marker, small notepad or sticky notes, and the white or yellow candle.

Light the candle, symbolizing the illumination of wisdom and courage brought forth by Athena. Allow its gentle flame to create a serene ambiance, inviting the goddess's guidance into the ritual.

Take a moment to center yourself, focusing on your breath. Inhale deeply, allowing the air to fill your lungs, and exhale slowly, releasing any tension or self-doubt. Set the intention to cultivate self-confidence and embrace your true beauty.

Hold the handheld mirror in your hands, looking into your own eyes. Affirm the following words or speak your own empowering affirmations:

"Athena, goddess of wisdom and courage,
I invoke your presence within me.
As I gaze into the mirror, I see my true strength.
I am confident, powerful, and deserving of love.
With gratitude, I embrace my true beauty."

Place the mirror on a stable surface, facing you. Take the pen or marker and the small notepad or sticky notes, and write down empowering affirmations that reflect your true worth and potential. Examples include "I am enough," "I embrace my uniqueness," or "I radiate confidence and inner beauty."

Place the affirmations strategically on the mirror's surface, surrounding your reflection. Each note serves as a reminder of your inner strength and positive self-image. Arrange them in a way that resonates with you, creating a visually empowering display.

Stand or sit in front of the mirror, observing your reflection surrounded by the empowering affirmations. Take a moment to absorb the words, allowing them to penetrate your consciousness and uplift your spirit.

Lightly touch each affirmation as you repeat it aloud or silently in your mind. Feel the power of the words resonating within you, replacing self-doubt with self-assurance and nurturing a positive self-image.

As you gaze into the mirror, affirm your strength, beauty, and worthiness. Speak words of self-love and empowerment, reminding yourself of your unique qualities and the impact you have on the world.

Take your time to reflect upon the empowering affirmations, fully embracing their meaning and significance. Let the light of the candle and the energy of Athena's wisdom infuse your thoughts with clarity and confidence.

When you feel ready, express gratitude to Athena for her guidance and the newfound self-confidence that has emerged. Acknowledge the strength and beauty that reside within you, knowing that you are capable of great things.

Extinguish the candle, symbolizing the completion of the empowering mirror affirmations. Take a moment to appreciate the transformation that has taken place and the positive energy that now radiates from within you.

As you conclude this ritual honoring Athena and the inner strength she represents. Embrace the power of positive self-talk and the reflection of your true beauty. May this ritual continue to inspire self-confidence and nurture a positive self-image in all aspects of your life.

Carry the empowering affirmations with you, both within your heart and through physical reminders, allowing them to uplift and empower you on your journey. Whenever doubt or self-criticism arises, return to the mirror and the affirmations, reminding yourself of your inherent worth and strength.

Incorporate these empowering affirmations into your daily routine. Each time you encounter your reflection in the mirror, take a moment to repeat the affirmations and reinforce your positive self-image. Allow them to permeate your thoughts and actions, guiding you with confidence and grace.

Remember that self-empowerment is an ongoing journey. Embrace the growth and transformation that comes with embracing your true beauty and inner strength. Trust in yourself and your abilities, knowing that you possess the wisdom and courage to navigate life's challenges.

May Athena's inspire you to stand tall, to celebrate your uniqueness, and to embrace your own brilliance. Shine your light brightly, for the world benefits from your empowered presence.

Garden of Gratitude

Introductory Section: In this ritual of gratitude and abundance, we connect with Demeter, the Greek goddess of harvest and fertility. Inspired by her nurturing energy, we create a gratitude garden to cultivate appreciation for the blessings in our lives and attract abundance.

Ritual Items:

Small plant or flowerpot

Soil

Seeds or small plant of your choice (such as herbs, flowers, or vegetables)

Decorative stones or crystals

Conducting the Ritual:

Find a peaceful and nurturing space where you can focus on gratitude and abundance. Gather the small plant or flowerpot, soil, seeds or small plant, and decorative stones or crystals.

Take a moment to center yourself, grounding your energy. Inhale deeply, connecting with the Earth's nurturing energy, and exhale slowly, releasing any tension or worries. Set the intention to cultivate gratitude and attract abundance into your life.

Hold the small plant or flowerpot in your hands, feeling the connection to nature and the energy of Demeter's harvest. Close your eyes and visualize the plant thriving and growing, symbolizing the abundance that you seek.

Open your eyes and place the soil in the pot, creating a nurturing bed for your gratitude garden. As you do so, express your gratitude to the Earth for providing the nourishment and support needed for growth.

Plant the seeds or plant in the soil, infusing each action with intentions of gratitude and abundance. Visualize these seeds or plant representing the blessings in your life that you are grateful for and wish to multiply.

Sprinkle decorative stones or crystals on top of the soil, symbolizing the abundance and prosperity you seek to attract. Each stone or crystal serves as a reminder of the blessings already present and the limitless potential for growth and abundance.

As you tend to your gratitude garden, water it with love and care. With each watering, express gratitude for the abundance in your life and visualize the blessings multiplying, just as the plant grows and flourishes.

Take a moment to reflect on the specific blessings and abundance you wish to cultivate. Express your gratitude for these blessings, both big and small, as you envision them expanding and manifesting in your life.

Place the gratitude garden in a location where it can receive sunlight and be a visible reminder of your blessings and abundance. Each time you see the garden, take a moment to appreciate the beauty and potential it represents.

As your gratitude garden grows, nurture it with love and gratitude. Take note of its progress, observing how your intentions and gratitude manifest in the flourishing growth of the plant.

Whenever you feel the need to cultivate gratitude or attract abundance, spend time with your gratitude garden. Touch the leaves, breathe in its fragrance, and express your appreciation for the blessings in your life.

Express gratitude to Demeter for her guidance and the abundant blessings she bestows.

Acknowledge the power of gratitude in cultivating abundance and fostering a deeper connection to the Earth's nurturing energy.

Through this ritual you honor Demeter and cultivate an attitude of gratitude and abundance. Embrace the power of gratitude to multiply blessings and attract abundance into your life. May your gratitude garden be a reminder of the abundance already present and the limitless potential for growth and joy.

With gratitude and an open heart, continue on your path of cultivating gratitude, nurturing abundance, and embracing the blessings in your life.

Melodic Muse

In this ritual we invoke the presence of Euterpe, the Greek muse of music and lyrical poetry. Inspired by her creative energy, we engage in the practice of playing musical instruments to cultivate harmony within ourselves and in our surroundings. This ritual can be done by yourself or with as many musicians as you wish, your instrument of choice could also be your voice, as it's our own built in musical instrument.

Ritual Items:

Your preferred musical instrument
Incense or smudging herbs
Comfortable seating or standing area
Optional: Crystals or gemstones for amplifying energy

Find a peaceful and serene space where you can focus on musical harmony and self-expression. Gather your musical instrument, incense or smudging herbs, comfortable seating or standing area, and optional crystals or gemstones.

Set the intention for creative expression, harmony, and inner resonance. Light the incense or smudge herbs, allowing the cleansing smoke to purify the space and create a sacred atmosphere.

Find a comfortable position in your chosen seating or standing area. Take a few deep breaths, allowing your body and mind to relax. Release any tension or distractions with each exhale, creating space for the melodic journey ahead.

Hold your musical instrument lovingly in your hands, feeling their energy and potential for creative expression. Take a moment to connect with the essence of Euterpe, the muse of music, and invite her presence into your practice.

Begin to play your instrument, allowing the melodies to flow freely from your heart. Let the music become an extension of your emotions, thoughts, and desires. Explore different rhythms, tones, and harmonies, following the intuitive guidance of your instrument.

As you immerse yourself in the melodies, close your eyes and surrender to the music's enchantment. Allow the vibrations to resonate within you, soothing your spirit, and bringing a sense of inner harmony and peace.

If you have chosen to use crystals or gemstones, hold them in your hands or place them near your musical instrument, allowing their energy to align with the harmonies you create. Visualize their energies merging with the music, amplifying the healing and transformative power.

Allow the music to carry you on a journey of self-expression and self-discovery. Embrace the emotions that arise as you play, allowing the melodies to flow effortlessly, transcending any limitations or inhibitions.

As you explore the sounds of your instrument, notice any areas of tension or imbalance within yourself. Use the music as a tool for release and healing, allowing the vibrations to dissolve energetic blockages and restore a sense of equilibrium.

Continue playing your instrument for as long as desired, losing yourself in the meditative and healing power of music. Trust your intuition and let the melodies guide you in this transformative experience.

Throughout the session, remain attuned to the subtleties of the music and its impact on your being. Observe any shifts in emotions, thoughts, or physical sensations, allowing the harmonies to bring balance and alignment to all aspects of your being.

When you feel ready to conclude the ritual, gradually bring your playing to a gentle close. Take a moment to appreciate the power of music and the connection you have cultivated with Euterpe, the muse of music.

As you complete this melodic harmony ritual, honor Euterpe and the creative energy she represents. Embrace the transformative and healing effects of music within your body, mind, and spirit. May the melodies you create continue to resonate within you, fostering harmony, self-expression, and inner resonance.

With gratitude and a deep appreciation for the power of music, carry the vibrations of melodic harmony with you, allowing them to uplift your spirit and bring harmony to your daily life. Whenever you feel the need for self-expression, relaxation, or inner balance, return to your instrument and engage in the practice of melodic harmony.

Acknowledge the unique gifts and talents that you bring to the world through your music. Embrace the creative flow that emerges from within and allow it to inspire and uplift not only yourself but also those around you.

Express gratitude to Euterpe for her presence and guidance throughout this melodic harmony ritual. Acknowledge the profound connection you have formed with the power of music and its ability to harmonize your inner being.

As you continue on your musical journey, let the melodies you create be a reflection of your true essence. Allow your instrument to become an extension of your soul, conveying emotions, stories, and experiences that transcend words.

May the harmonies you create with Euterpe's guidance resonate within your heart and echo through the world, bringing joy, healing, and inspiration to all who hear them. Embrace the transformative power of music and let it be a guiding force in your life.

With the music as your companion, walk the path of melodic harmony, sharing your unique melodies with love and authenticity. Let your instrument be a vessel for self-expression, creative exploration, and the cultivation of inner resonance.

Rhythms of Friendship

In this ritual we'll be invoking Freya, the Norse goddess of love, beauty, and friendship. Inspired by her joyful energy, we gather with our friends to embrace the power of music and dance, strengthening our bonds and creating lasting memories.

Ritual Items:

Sound system or music-playing device

Open and spacious area for dancing

Decorative elements (such as flowers or ribbons)

Optional: Refreshments or snacks to share

Choose a suitable location for your ritual, ensuring there is enough space for everyone to move and dance freely. Set up the sound system or music-playing device in a central position.

Decorate the space with your chosen decorative elements, incorporating elements of beauty and friendship. Consider using flowers, ribbons, or any other items that evoke a sense of joy and connection.

Invite your friends to join you in this ritual of friendship and celebration. Encourage them to bring their favorite dance moves, wear comfortable clothing, and come with open hearts and minds.

Before starting the music, gather in a circle with your friends. Take a moment to center yourselves and connect with the intention of celebrating friendship, unity, and the joy of movement.

As the ritual leader, initiate a brief meditation or breathing exercise to help everyone release any tensions or worries. Encourage deep, intentional breaths, allowing the breath to flow through the body and create a sense of inner calm.

After the grounding exercise, announce the start of the ritual by playing music that inspires joy and fosters connection. Choose songs that resonate with the spirit of Freya, embracing themes of love, beauty, and friendship.

As the music fills the space, let the dance floor become a sacred space of expression and togetherness. Encourage each person to move their bodies in ways that feel natural and authentic to them. Let go of inhibitions and surrender to the joyful energy of Freya.

Engage in spontaneous group dances, duets, or solo performances—anything that brings laughter, joy, and a sense of camaraderie. Embrace the spirit of Freya as you dance with your friends, celebrating the beauty of friendship and the connections you share.

Take moments throughout the ritual to make eye contact with your friends, smiling and acknowledging the shared experience. Let the music and movement deepen your connection, fostering a sense of unity and reinforcing the bonds of friendship.

Dance with passion and enthusiasm, allowing the music to guide your movements. Let your body become an expression of joy, love, and freedom. Encourage one another to fully embrace the dance, celebrating each other's unique rhythms and styles.

Embrace moments of collaboration and improvisation, where friends can dance together, creating synchronized movements or mirroring each other's steps. Celebrate the beauty of co-creation and the harmonious energy that arises from shared dance.

As the ritual draws to a close, gradually transition into a slower, more reflective song. Gather in a circle once again, holding hands or placing hands on each other's shoulders. Express gratitude to Freya for her presence and the transformative power of dance and friendship.

Take a moment to honor and appreciate the connections you have with each other, acknowledging the love, support, and joy that your friendships bring to your lives.

May the dance of friendship, guided by the spirit of Freya, continue to resonate within you and strengthen the bonds of camaraderie. Embrace the power of music and movement as catalysts for connection, joy, and celebration in your lives.

In Closing

As we come to the end of this journey through the realms of manifestation, harmony, and positivity, I'd like to extend my heartfelt gratitude for joining me on this path of jubilance, love, and harmony. Throughout this book, we have explored a myriad of rituals designed to uplift, empower, and bring forth the beauty of the feminine energies within us all. It's my sincere hope that you have found inspiration, joy, and a deep connection to the magic that resides within you.

Adaptation is the key to unlocking the full potential of these rituals. Feel free to modify and personalize them to better align with your own intentions, desires, and beliefs. You may choose to work with different goddesses or mythological beings that resonate with you on a deeper level. Trust your intuition and allow your unique path to unfold as you infuse each ritual with your own essence.

Additionally, the ritual items suggested are mere tools to aid in your journey. They can be interchanged, added to, or removed as you see fit. The most important element is the intention you bring to each ritual. Your intention, fueled by love, belief, and clarity, is the true catalyst for manifestation and transformation.

As you continue your magical exploration, remember that magic is not confined to the rituals within these pages. It is a mindset, a way of embracing life with an open heart, seeking beauty, joy, and harmony in every experience. It is an invitation to infuse the world around you with the enchantment of love and positivity.

May the rituals you have encountered in this book continue to guide you on your path of growth, empowerment, and love. May the wisdom of the goddess be ever-present in your heart, nurturing your spirit and radiating out into the world.

Infinite Love and Blessings,
Brittany Nightshade

Merry met!

And merry part!

-Brittany Nightshade

Disclaimer: Always take safety precautions when doing any ritual. Be careful if using stoves or any heat sources and always make sure to have proper ventilation. This information is educational and religious, it is not to be taken as professional medical advice, always consult with a medical professional first and foremost. Use this book at your own peril: I'm not responsible for any unintended consequences. Never ingest anything unless you're completely sure it's safe and you aren't allergic. Always be wary of the potential risk of forcing your will onto others, as there can be unintended consequences. Do not commit any crimes, such as trespassing, when conducting your rituals: I don't have a spell to get you out of jail!

Much love,
Brittany

If you've enjoyed the book, please consider giving me a review on Amazon and following me on Instagram and Facebook:

facebook.com/xobrittanynightshade

@Nightshade_Apothecary

www.ingramcontent.com/pod-product-compliance
Lightning Source LLC
Chambersburg PA
CBHW051853130726
47987CB00002B/819